Eyewitness Accounts of the American Revolution

Private Journal Kept During the Revolutionary War

Margaret Morris

The New York Times & Arno Press

PRIVATE JOURNAL

KEPT

DURING A PORTION OF THE

REVOLUTIONARY WAR,

FOR THE AMUSEMENT OF A SISTER.

BY

MARGARET MORRIS.

OF BURLINGTON, N. J.

PHILADELPHIA:

PRIVATELY PRINTED.

1836.

INTRODUCTION.

HE following brief journal, embracing all that has been pre-
served of a manuscript much valued by the descendants of the,
writer, is now printed for their perusal. Though it may interest the antiquarian and historian of a future day, it is not
designed for the public, and *but fifty copies* have been printed
thus confining its circulation within a narrow compass.

But very few, if any, similar journals kept during the same
period, are believed to exist; and as it details the daily alarms
to which a private family was liable, the frequent, and often
absurd reports circulated, and the kind of persecution to which obnoxious indi-
viduals were subjected; it will serve as a picture, *in little,* of the times.

Of the writer, Margaret Morris, it will be sufficient to state that she was a
member of the Society of Friends; was left a widow early in life, and died in
1816, at Burlington, N. J., at the age of seventy-nine. Her maiden name was
Hill; her father, Richard Hill, was extensively engaged in the Madeira wine
trade, and resided with his large family in that island for a considerable period.
Her brother, Henry Hill, of the firm of Hill, Bissett & Co., accumulated a large
fortune in the same business, and died of yellow fever, without descendants, at

his residence, in Fourth street, Philadelphia, since occupied by Dr. P. S. Physick. She was a pious Christian; her ever cheerful and equable temperament, through many years of great suffering and confinement to her couch, were truly remarkable; it is in that character that she is best remembered by her grand-children and numerous connections, to whom her whole career was a pattern of modesty, benevolence, and a just reliance on Divine Providence, which never failed to sustain her through many trials.

No apology is offered for her political feelings; those she possessed in common with too many of her countrymen, both good and great, to make her a mark for satire or reprehension. The few domestic circumstances that occur, are left as I found them, believing that they add to the interest of the journal, in which scarcely an alteration has been made, except to insert a name or an initial where the persons alluded to were left in uncertainty. It is much to be regretted that the manuscript is so brief, but it is not, on that account, unworthy of preservation. The sister for whom the journal was written, was Milcah Martha Moore, wife of Dr. Charles Moore, then residing at Montgomery Square, Pa.

To the descendants of the estimable lady, whose cheerful and religious mind they portray, these few pages are dedicated by her grand-son,

Philadelphia, 1836.   JOHN J. SMITH, Jr.

PRIVATE JOURNAL.

DEC. 6th, 1776. Being on a visit to my friend, M. S., at Haddonfield, I was preparing to return to my family, when a person from Philadelphia told me the people there were in great commotion,—that the English fleet was in the river, and hourly expected to sail up to the city,—that the inhabitants were removing into the country,—and that several persons of considerable repute had been discovered to have formed a design of setting fire to the city, and were summoned before the congress and strictly enjoined to drop the horrid purpose. When I heard the above report my heart almost died within me, and I cried, surely the Lord will not punish the innocent with the guilty, and I wished there might be found some interceding Lots and Abrahams amongst *our people*. On my journey home, I was told the inhabitants of our little town [Burlington, N. J.] were going in haste into the country, and that my nearest neighbours were already removed. When I heard this, I felt myself quite sick; I was ready to faint—I thought of my S. D. [Sarah Dillwynn, wife of George, then absent,] the beloved companion of my widowed state—her husband at the distance of some hundred miles from her—I thought of my own lonely situation, no husband to cheer with the voice of love my sinking spirits. My little flock, too, without a father to direct them how to steer. All these things crowded into my mind at once, and I felt like one forsaken; a flood of friendly tears came to my relief, and I felt a humble confidence that He who had been with me in six troubles, would not forsake me now. While I cherished this hope, my tranquility was restored, and I felt no sensations but of humble acquiescence to the Divine will—and was favoured to find my family in good health on my arrival, and my dear companion not greatly discomposed, for which favour I desire to be truly thankful.

Dec. 7th.   A letter from my next neighbour's husband, at the camp, warned her to be gone in haste, and many persons coming into town to day, brought intelligence that the British army were advancing towards us.

Dec. 8th.   Every day begins and ends with the same accounts, and we hear to-day, that the regulars are at Trenton—some of our neighbours gone, and others going, makes our little bank [Green Bank on the river,] look lonesome. But our trust in Providence still firm, and we dare not even talk of removing our family.

Dec. 9th.   This evening were favoured with the company of our faithful friend and brother, R. W. [Rd. Wells.] This testimony of his love, was truly acceptable to us.

Dec. 10th.   To-day our amiable friend, E. C. [Hetty Cox] and her family bade us adieu. My brother also left us, but returned in less than an hour, telling us, he could not go away just as the Hessians were entering the town—but no troops coming in, we urged him to leave us next morning, which he concluded to do after preparing us to expect the Hessians in a few hours. A number of galleys have been lying in the river, before the town, for two days past.

Dec. 11th.   After various reports from one hour to another, of light-horse approaching, the people in town had certain intelligence that a large body of Hessians were come to Bordentown, and we might expect to see them in a few hours. About 10 o'clock of this day, a party of about 60 men marched down the main street —as they passed along they told our doctor [Odell,] and some other persons in the town, that a large number of Hessians were advancing, and would be in the town in less than an hour. This party were riflemen, who, it seems, had crossed the river somewhere in the neighbourhood of Bordentown, to reconnoitre, and meeting with a superior number of Hessians on the road, were then returning, and took Burlington in their way back; from us they crossed to Bristol, and by the time they were fairly embarked, the Hessians, to the number, as we heard, of 4 or 500, had passed, what we call, York bridge. On the first certainty of their approach, Jno. Lawrence and two or three others thought best, for the safety of the town, to go out and meet the troops. He communicated his intention to one of the gondola captains, who approved of it and desired to be informed of the result.

The gentlemen went out, and though the Hessian colonel spoke but little English, yet they found that upon being thus met in a peaceable manner on behalf of the inhabitants, he was ready to promise them safety and security, to exchange any messages that might be proper with the gentlemen of the galleys. In the meantime he ordered his troops to halt; they remained in their ranks between the bridge and the corner of Main street, waiting an answer from on board. J. L. and T. H. went down to report what had passed, and told Capt. Moore that the colonel had orders to quarter his troops in Burlington that night, and that if the inhabitants were quiet and peaceable, and would furnish him with quarters and refreshment, he would pledge his honour that no manner of disorder should happen to disturb or alarm the people. Capt. Moore replied, that in his opinion it would be wrong in such a case

to fire on the town, but that he would go down and consult with
the commodore, and return an answer as soon as might be. While
this answer was waited for, Dr. Odell was told it would be a satisfaction, both to the Hessian commandant and to our own people,
to have a person who could serve as interpreter between them—
not doubting the foreigner could speak French, the doctor went
to him, and he had the satisfaction to find it probable, at least,
that he might be of service to the people of the town. The commandant seemed highly pleased to find a person with whom he
could converse with ease and precision.

He desired the doctor to tell the gentlemen of the town to the
same purport as above, with this addition—that he expected there
would be found no persons in the town in arms; nor any arms,
ammunition or effects, belonging to persons that were in arms
against the king, concealed by any of the inhabitants; that if any
such effects were thus secreted, the house in which they were found
would be given up to pillage; to prevent which, it would be necessary to give him a just and fair account of such effects, which
account he would forward to the general, and that if we acted
openly and in good faith in these respects, he repeated his assur-
ances, upon the honour of a soldier, that he would be answerable
for every kind of disorder on the part of his troops. They remained
in profound silence in their ranks, and the commandant with some
of his officers came into town as far as J. L.'s, where they dined,
waiting the commodore's answer.

The doctor says, that as he thought he observed much of the
gentleman in the commandant, and the appearance, at least, of
generosity and humanity, he took an opportunity to inform him,
that there was an old friend of his [the Dr.'s] who was a colonel,
and of some estimation in the continental army—that he was at
present with Gen. Washington, and that his lady, an amiable
woman, had gone into the country with most of her effects—that

the doctor was ignorant of the place of her retreat, but that before her departure she had begged him on the footing of former friendship to take into his house, and if he might be permitted to keep as under his protection, some few things which she could not remove, and told the commandant, he was ready to give an exact account of such of her effects as he had thus taken charge of; and at the same time confessed that when he took them, it was in the hope of being suffered to preserve them for his friend. The commandant told him without a moment's hesitation, "Sir, you need not be at the trouble of giving any further account of those things you have so candidly mentioned—be assured that whatever effects have been entrusted with you in this way, I shall consider as your own, and they shall not be touched." From this answer he was encouraged to hope he might be of still further service to his friends, and in the full persuasion that nothing would occur to disturb the peaceable disposition that was making; but as it happened the commodore had received intelligence of a party of Hessians having entered Burlington before Captain Moore got down to him, and had ordered up four galleys to fire on the town wherever any two or three persons should be seen together. Capt. Moore met and hailed them one after another, but the wind was so high that he was not heard or not understood. The four gondolas came up, and the first of them appearing before the main street, J. L., T. H. and W. D.* went down upon the wharf and waved a hat, the signal agreed on with Capt. Moore for the boat to come ashore and give the commodore's answer in peace; to the astonishment of these gentlemen, all the answer they received was first a swivel shot. Not believing it possible this could be designedly done, they stood still, and J. L. again waved his hat, and was answered with an 18 pounder; both these fires as the gondola people have since

---

*Wm. Dillwyn, married to a sister of Jno. Smith, father of Susan Emlen, and afterwards settled in England.

told us, were made with as good aim as could be taken, as they took it for granted it was at Hessians they fired ; however, as it was impossible to conjecture that such conduct could have happened, or to suspect such a mistake, it is no wonder the town was exceedingly alarmed ; looking upon it in the light of a cruel as well as unprovoked piece of treachery. Upon this news, the commandant rose calmly from table, and his officers with him went out to eight or ten men, who had come to the door as a small bodyguard—he turned to the doctor as he went into the street, and said, he could easily dispose of his people out of the possibility of danger, but that much mischief might be done to the town, and that he would take a view of the gondolas, and see what measures might be necessary on his part ; but that he should be sorry to be the occasion of any damage or distress to the inhabitants. He walked down the street, and sent different ways three sentinels in Indian file together—to view and report to him what they saw.

These being now and then seen at different times, induced the people on board to believe that the houses were full of Hessians, and a cannonade was continued till almost dark, in different directions, sometimes along the street, sometimes across it. Several houses were struck, and a little damaged, but not one living creature, either man or beast, killed or wounded. About dark the gondolas fell down a little way below the town, and the night was passed in quiet.

While all this tumult was in town, we, on our peaceful bank, ignorant of the occasion of the firing, were wondering what it could mean, and unsuspecting of danger, were quietly pursuing our business in the family, when a kind neighbour informed us of the occasion, and urged us to go into the cellar, as a place of safety. We were prevailed on by him to do so, and remained there till it ceased.

Dec. 12th. The people of the galleys, suspecting that some

troops were yet either concealed in the town or neighbourhood of it, have been very jealous of the inhabitants, who have often been alarmed with reports that the city would be set on fire ; many have gone in haste and great distress into the country, but we still hope no mischief is seriously intended. A number of men landed on our bank this morning, and told us it was their settled purpose to set fire to the town. I begged them not to set my house on fire ; they asked which was my house, and they said they knew not what hindered them from firing on it last night, for seeing a light in the chambers they thought there were Hessians in it, and they pointed their guns at it several times. I told them my children were sick, which obliged me to burn a light all night. Though they did not know what hindered them from firing on us I did ; it was the guardian of the widow and the orphan, who took us into his safe-keeping, and preserved us from danger ;—oh, that I may keep humble, and be thankful for this, as well as other favours vouchsafed to my little flock.

Dec. 13th. This day we began to look a little like ourselves again. The troops were removed some miles from town, as we hear, and our friends began to venture out to see us—but the suspicions of the gondola men, still continued, and search was made in and about the town for men distinguished by the name of tories. About noon of this day dear brother R. W. popped in upon us—he had heard the firing yesterday, and being anxious for our safety, he ran the risk of venturing amongst us to see how we had fared— surely this proof of his love will never be forgotten by me while my memory lasts : he left us after dinner.

Dec. 14. This day there was no appearance of the formidable Hessians. Several of our friends called to see us ; amongst the number was one (Dr. Odell,) esteemed by the whole family, and very intimate in it ; but the spirit of the devil still continued to rove through the town in the shape of tory-hunters. A message was delivered to our intimate friend, informing him a party of armed men were on the search for him—his horse was brought, and he retired to a place of safety. Some of the gentlemen, who entertained the foreigners, were pointed out to the gondola men— two worthy inhabitants* were seized upon, and dragged on board.

From the 13th to the 16th, we had various reports of the advancing and retiring of the enemy; parties of armed men rudely entered the town, and diligent search was made for tories: some of the gondola gentry broke into and pillaged Rd. Smith's house on the bank. Mem. To give a more particular account of the manner by and by. About noon this day, [16th,] a very terrible account of thousands coming into town, and now actually to be seen on Gallows Hill—my incautious son† caught up the spy-glass, and was running towards the mill to look at them. I told him it would be liable to misconstruction, but he prevailed on me to allow him to gratify his curiosity—he went, but returned much dissatisfied, for no troops could he see—as he came back poor Dick‡ took the glass, and resting it against a tree, took a view of the fleet—both of these were observed by the people on board, who suspected it was an enemy that was watching their motions. They manned a boat, and sent her on shore—a loud knocking at my door brought me to it—I was a little fluttered, and kept locking and unlocking that I might get my ruffled face a little composed—at last I opened it, and half a dozen men all armed, demanded the key of the empty house. I asked what they wanted there; they said to search for a d—d tory who had been spying at them from the mill. The name of a tory, so near *my own door*, seriously alarmed me, for a poor *refugee*, dignified by that name, had claimed the shelter of my roof, and was at that very time concealed like a thief in an

*Rd. Smith, &c.
†Dr. Jno. Morris.
‡Rd. Hill Morris.

auger hole—I rung the bell violently, the signal agreed on if they came to search, and when I thought he had crept into the hole, I put on a very simple look, and cried out, " Bless me, I hope you are not Hessians." " Do we look like Hessians," asked one of them, rudely. " Indeed I don't know." " Did you never see a Hessian ?" " No, never in my life ; but they are *men*, and you are men, and may be Hessians, for anything I know—but I'll go with you into Col. Cox's house, though indeed it was my son at the mill ; he is but a boy, and meant no harm—he wanted to see the troops."

So I marched at the head of them, opened the door, and searched every place, but we could not find the tory,—strange where he could be. We returned—they, greatly disappointed—I, pleased ̄ to think my house was not suspected. The captain, a smart little fellow, named Shippen, said he wished he could see the spy-glass. S. D. produced it, and very civilly desired his acceptance of it, which I was sorry for, as I often amused myself in looking through it. They left us, and searched J V.'s [James Verree] and the two next houses, but no tory could they find. This transaction reached the town, and Colonel Cox was very angry, and ordered the men on board. In the evening I went to town with my refugee, and placed him in other lodgings. I was told to-day of a design to seize upon a young man in town, as he was esteemed a tory. I thought a hint would be kindly received, and, as I came back, called upon a friend of his, and told him. Next day he was out of the reach of the gondolas.

Dec. 17th. More news ! great news ! very great news ; [J. V.'s]. The British troops actually at Mount Holly !—guards of militia placed at London and York bridges—gondola men in arms patrolling the street, and diligent search making for fire-arms, ammunition, and tories—another attempt last night to enter into R. Smith's house. Early this morning J. V. sent in, to beg I would let my son go a few miles out of town on some business for him. I consented, not knowing of the formidable doings up town—when I heard of it I felt a mother's pangs for her son all the day ; but when night came, and he did not appear, I made no doubt of his being taken by the Hessians. A friend made my mind easy, by telling me he had passed through the town where the dreadful Hessians were said to be "playing the very mischief," (J. V. again) ; it is certain there were numbers of them at Mount Holly, but they behaved very civilly to the people, excepting only a few persons, who were actually in rebellion, as they termed it, whose goods, &c., they injured. This evening every gondola man sent on board, with strict orders not to set a foot on the Jersey shore again—so far so good.

Dec. 18th. This morning gives us hope of a quiet day—but my mind still anxious for my son, not yet returned. Our refugee gone off to-day out of the reach of gondolas and tory hunters—much talk of the enemy—two Hessians had the assurance to appear in town to-day ; they asked if there were any rebels in town, and desired to be shown the *men of war*—what a burlesque on *men of war !* My son returned to night, and to his mortification saw not one Hessian, light-horse, or anything else worth seeing, but had the consolation of a little adventure at York Bridge, being made to give an account of himself as he went out yesterday, his horse detained, and he ordered to walk back to town and get a pass from Gen. Reed ; this he readily agreed to, but instead of a pass, Col. Cox accompanied him back to the bridge, and Don Quixote, jr., mounted his horse, and rode through their ranks in triumph. Two field pieces said to be mounted at Bristol.

Dec. 19th. A man was met on the road, with a white flag or rag tied to a stick, but whence he came, or where he was going, the wisest head on the bank [J. V.] cannot conjecture. A report prevails, that Gen. Putnam with 1000 men are on their march—

this put all into motion at Holly. The Hessians retire to the Black-Horse. Not one gondola man ashore all this day ; we may burn a candle all night and sleep secure. This evening received a letter from Dr. C. M. [Charles Moore], inviting me to move into his neighbourhood, but my mind is easiest while I conclude to abide where Providence has cast my lot—he has preserved us in great dangers, and I dare not distrust his future care. A letter from the brother and friend of my heart [Geo. Dillwyn], gives me hope of his return ; his advice must determine my future movements.

Dec. 20th. A snow storm last night has almost stopped the navigation, and sent our guarda-costas out of our sight down the river ; surely this will be a quiet day—methinks I will call for my work-basket, and set myself to sewing—but hark! a rap at the door—that face [J. V.] is full of intelligence. " Well, what news, neighbour ?" " Oh, bless me! great news, indeed! why, ha'nt your heard it ?" " No, we have seen nobody from town to-day ; do tell us." " Why, the Hessians are actually just here ; Master P., W. D., &c., &c., are all gone out to see what they can do." " Well! and will they bring them all into town? I'm sure we are but poorly provided just now for a great deal of company." J. V. still goes on—" Oh! Ah! you will have enough of them ; I expect to have my house full! I saw a man from Holly, yesterday, who says he saw fifty of the light-horse, all very fine English horses —oh it was a terrible sight to see how they all foamed at the mouth and pranced—and fifty Hessians all quartered at Holly ; but Putnam is surely coming with 150C men." " Well, but neighbour, I should suppose it was a very fine sight to see so many fine horses together, and prancing."—" Oh no, bless my spirits! it is a terrible sight to see how they foamed at the mouth !" " Well, we shall hear by and by what the ambassadors have done—I hope they won't come in to night with the Hessians, for I am quite unprovided to entertain company." (Observe, Patty, it was I that was in such a fidget and not provided for company).—" Whip the fellows, I got supper enough for twenty of them the first night of the alarm, and I'm resolved I'll trouble myself no more about them till I see some of them in earnest—17 Hessians in town to-day, and we were told the Recorder was desired to prepare a dinner for about 500 men—a friend, from town, called in about 4 o'clock, and told us they were all a-coming. We asked if he had seen them? no! but he heard they were just here—we asked him how we, at this distance from town, should know of their coming; they might pop upon us here and scare us out of our wits—as we had no man in the house—he said, " Oh, you will know of it fast enough, I warrant—why the noise of the cannon and wagons will be heard at a great distance, and I advise you to make good use of your time till they do come, and put all things of gold and silver out of their way, and all linen too, or you will lose it." I said they pillaged none but rebels, and we were not such; we had taken no part against them, &c. But that signified nothing; we should lose all, &c. After he was gone, my S. D. and myself asked each other why it was that all these stories did not put us into a fright— we were not even discomposed; surely it is a favour never to be forgotten. We concluded to sit up a little later than usual tonight, but no rattling could we hear. Ambassadors returned—a report that the congress dollars will be allowed to circulate for a certain number of years—a battery talked of, to be raised at the point of the island. We are told the two pieces of cannon, said to be at Bristol, have disappeared.

Dec. 21st. More snow last night—no danger of gondolas now —more ambassadors gone out to-day to the Hessians—not much to be expected from one of them. A great deal of talk in the neighbourhood about a neutral island; wish with great earnestness it may be allowed—wonder the men in town don't think it worth

while to step down here and tell us what they are after—get quite
in the fidgets for news—send Dick to town to collect some—he
returns quite newsless—good mind to send him back again. W.
D. comes at last—tells us all we expected to hear—pleases us by
saying we shall have timely notice of their coming—gives a hint
that the feeble and defenceless will find safety and protection—
rank ourselves among the number, having no man with us in the
house. Determine not to be unprovided again, let them come or
not, as the weather is now so cold provisions will keep good several days. We pity the poor fellows who were obliged to be out
last night in the snow. Repeat our wishes that this may be a
neutral island—quite sleepy—go to bed and burn a lamp all night
—talk as loud as usual, and don't regard the creaking of the door
no gondola men listening about the bank. Before we retired to
bed this evening, an attempt was made to teach the children to
pronounce " *vegates*," (how do you do?) like a Dutchman. Our
good neighbour a little concerned to think there is not one in the
neighbourhood that will be able to interpret for us when the Hessians are quartered on us. At last, by dint of mere conjuration,
I discover that his maid is a Dutch woman, and we resolve, *nem.
con.*, that she shall be the interpreter of the bank, and her master
thinks it will be a great thing to have one that can speak for us.

Dec. 22d. It is said Putnam with 1000 men are at Mount
Holly ; all the women removed from the town, except one widow
of our acquaintance—this evening we hear the sound of much
hammering at Bristol, and it is conjectured that a fortification is
carrying on there—more cannon said to be planted on the island—
we hear this afternoon that the gentlemen who went last to the
Count de Nope with a request that our town might be allowed to
remain a neutral one, are returned, and report that he had too
many affairs of greater consequence in hand to attend to them, or
give an answer. I think we don't like the Count quite so well to-

day, as we did yesterday. We heard yesterday that Gen. Lee was taken prisoner by a party of light-horse, who surrounded him, and took him to New York, (hope privately that he will not escape); to day (22d) we hear Gen. Howe is at Trenton, and it is thought there will be an engagement soon. A man who was at Mount Holly the other day, tells us he saw a great many of the British troops—that some of them went to the magazine there [a small room over the court-house] and took out about 100 wooden canteens, and the same number of broken fire-arms, and, calling for a guard of 100 men, piled them up in the street, and ordered the men in derision to take charge of them. This afternoon we hear of our refugee again, and that he has got a protection, as it is called. The rage of tory-hunting a little subsided; we now hear only of the Hessian-hunters; but they make a poor hand of it—not one brought in that we know of. We hear this afternoon that our officers are afraid their men will not fight and wish they may all run home again. A peaceable man ventured to prophesy to-day that, if the war is continued through the winter, the British troops will be scared at the sight of our men, for as they never fought with naked men, the novelty of it will terrify them, and make them retreat faster than they advanced to meet them; for he says, from the present appearance of our ragged troops, he thinks it probable they will not have clothes to cover them a month or two hence.

Several of the families, who left the town on the day of the cannonading, are returned to their houses; the intelligence brought in this evening is seriously affecting; a party of our men, about 200, marched out of Mount Holly, and meeting with a party of Hessians near a place called Petticoat Bridge, an engagement ensued—the Hessians retreating rather than advancing — a heavy firing of musketry and some cannon heard; we are informed that twenty-one of our men were killed in the engagement, and that they returned at night to their headquarters at Mount Holly, the Hessians to theirs at the Black Horse.

Dec. 23d. This day twelve gondolas came up the river again, but we know not as yet the occasion of their coming; the troops at Mount Holly went out again to day and engaged the Hessians near the same place where they met yesterday; it is reported we lost ten men, and that our troops are totally routed and the Hessians in possession of Mount Holly. This evening a little alarm in our neighborhood; a report reaching us that 3000 troops now at Bristol, are to cross over in the night, and to land on our bank in order to join the routed party of yesterday; my dear S. D.'s spirits for the first time forsook her on hearing this, and my heart grieved that I could offer nothing to compose her. We conjecture the gondolas are to lie here in readiness to receive our men should they be put to flight—be that as it may, we don't like to see them so near us, and wish for another snow storm to drive them away.

Dec. 24th. The gondolas all gone out of sight—but whether up or down the river we know not. This morning we are told of a fearful alarm which was spread through the town last night: that the gondolas had orders to fire on it in the night, as it was said the Hessians were expected to come in after the rout of yesterday, and take possession here as they had done at Mount Holly; happily this account did not reach us till it was proved to be false. It seems the commodore had sent one McKnight on shore, who informed the inhabitants of it. W. Smith and B. Helm went to Bristol in the evening, and acquainted Gen. Cadwallader with what they had heard, who signified to the commodore the necessity of the removal of the fleet, as the ice would probably make it difficult for them to sail a few days hence; when this was taken to the commodore, he denied having sent the information which so alarmed the inhabitants. It was thought he appeared a little disguised with liquor at the time. We hear the Hessians are still at

Holly, and our troops in possession of Church Hill, a little beyond; the account of twenty-one killed the first day of the engagement, and ten the next, is not to be depended on, as the Hessians say our men ran so fast they had not the opportunity of killing any of them. Several Hessians in town to day. They went to Daniel Smith's and enquired for several articles in the shop which they offered to pay for; two were observed to be in liquor in the street; they went to the tavern, and calling for rum ordered the man to charge it to the King. We hear that two houses in the skirts of the town were broke open by the Hessians and pillaged. The gondolas have been lying down at Dunk's Ferry all this day. A pretty heavy firing heard up the river to-day, but no account yet received of the occasion, or where it was.

Dec. 25th. An officer said to be gone to Bristol from the Count de Nope with a flag, and offers of letting our town remain a neutral post. Gen. Reed at Philadelphia. An express sent to him, and we hear he is to meet the Count to-morrow, at Jno. Antrim's, and settle the preliminaries.

Dec. 26th. Very stormy; we fear Gen. Reed will not meet the Count to-day. A great number of flat-bottom boats gone up the river; we cannot learn where they are going to.

Dec. 27th. A letter from Gen. Reed to his brother, informing him that Washington had had an engagement with the regulars, on the 25th, early in the morning, taking them by surprise; killed 50 and took 900 prisoners—the loss on our side not known, or if known, not suffered to be public. It seems this heavy loss to the regulars, was owing to the prevailing custom among the Hessians, of getting drunk on the eve of that great day which brought peace on earth, and good will to men—but oh! how unlike Christians is the manner in which they celebrate it. Can we call ourselves Christians, while we act so contrary to our master's rules? He set the example which we profess to follow, and here is a recent instance that we only profess it; instead of good will, envy and hatred seem to be the ruling passions in the breasts of thousands. This evening, the 27th, about 3000 of the Pennsylvania militia and other troops landed in the neck, and marched into town with artillery, baggage, &c., and are quartered on the inhabitants. One company were lodged at J. V.'s and a guard placed between his house and ours; we were so favoured as not to have any sent to our house. An officer spent the evening with us, and appeared to be in high spirits, and talked of engaging the English as a very trifling affair—nothing so easy as to drive them over the North River, &c.; not considering there is a God of battle, as well as a God of peace, who may have given them the late advantage, in order to draw them out to meet the chastisement that is reserved for them.

Dec. 28th. Early this morning the troops marched out of town in high spirits; a flight of snow this morning drove the gondolas again down the river. My heart sinks when I think of the numbers unprepared for death, who will probably be sent in a few days to appear before the Judge of Heaven. The weather clearing up this afternoon, we observed several boats, with soldiers and their baggage, making up to our wharf; as I looked at them, I thought I saw a face that was not strange to me, and taking a nearer view, found it was the well known face of my beloved brother and friend, G. Dillwyn. When I saw the companions he was among, I thought of what Solomon said of his beloved—that she was like an apple tree amongst the trees of the wood. When he came into the house, my kindred heart bade him welcome to the hospitable roof,—for so must I ever deem that roof which has sheltered me and my little flock,—though our joy at meeting him was checked by the prospect before and around. A man, who seemed to have command over the soldiers just landed, civilly asked for the keys of Col. Cox's house, in which they stowed their baggage, and took up their quarters for the night, and were very quiet.

Dec. 29th.   This morning the soldiers at the next house prepared to depart, and as they passed my door, they stopped to bless and thank me for the food I sent them, which I received, not as my due, but as belonging to my *master*, who had reached a morsel to them by my hand.   A great number of soldiers in town to day—another company took possession of the next house when the first left it.   The inhabitants much straightened for bread to supply the soldiers and fire-wood to keep them warm.   This seems to be only one of the many calamities of war.

Dec. 30th.   A number of poor soldiers sick and wounded brought into town to-day, and lodged in the court-house; some of them in private houses.   To-day I hear several of our townsmen have agreed to procure wood for the soldiers; but they found it was attended with considerable difficulty, as most of the wagons usually employed to bring in wood were pressed to take the soldiers' baggage

Dec. 31st.   We have been told of an engagement between the two armies, in which it was said the English had 400 taken prisoners, and 300 killed and wounded.   The report of the evening contradicts the above intelligence, and there is no certain account of a battle.

Jan. 1st. 1777.   This New Year's day has not been ushered in with the usual rejoicings, and I believe it will be the beginning of a sorrowful year to very many people.   Yet the flatterer, hope, bids me look forward with confidence to Him who can bring out of this confusion the greatest order.   I do not hear that any messengers have been in town from the camp.

Jan. 3d.   This morning we heard very distinctly a heavy firing of cannon ; the sound came from about Trenton, and at noon a number of soldiers, upwards of 1000, came into town in great confusion, with baggage and some cannon.   From these soldiers we learn there was a smart engagement yesterday, at Trenton, and that they left them engaged near Trenton mill, but were not able to say which side was victorious. They were again quartered on the inhabitants, and we again exempt from the cumber of having them lodged in our house. Several of those who lodged in Col. Cox's house last week, returned to night, and asked for the key, which I gave them; about bed time, I went into the next house to see if the fires were safe, and my heart was melted to see such a number of my fellow-creatures, lying like swine on the floor, fast asleep, and many of them without even a blanket to cover them. It seems very strange to me, that such a number should be allowed to come from the camp at the very time of the engagements, and I shrewdly suspect they have run away—for they can give no account why they came, nor where they are to march next.

Jan. 4th. The accounts hourly coming in, are so contradictory and various, that we know not which to give credit to. We have heard our people have gained another victory—that the English are fleeing before them, some at Brunswick, some at Princeton. We hear to day that Sharp Delany, and A. Morris, and others of the Pennsylvania militia, are killed, and that the Count de Nope is numbered with the dead; if so, the Hessians have lost a brave and humane commander. The prisoners taken by our troops, are sent to Lancaster jail. A number of sick and wounded brought into town—calls upon me to extend a hand of charity towards them. Several of *my* soldiers left the next house, and returned to the place from whence they came; upon my questioning them pretty close, I brought several to confess they had run away, being scared at the heavy firing on the 3d. There were several pretty innocent-looking lads among them, and I sympathised with their mothers, when I saw them preparing to return to the army.

Jan. 5th. I heard to-day that Capt. Shippen, who threatened to shoot my son for spying at the gondolas, is killed. I forgave him, long ago, for the fright he occasioned me, and felt sorry when I heard he was dead. We are told to-day that Gen. Mercer is killed, and Mifflin wounded; what sad havoc will this dreadful war make in our land!

Jan. 6th. We are told to day that 2000 New England men fell in the late engagement.

Jan. 7th. This evening all the gondolas, which have been for several days past lying before Bristol, sailed down the river, except one which is stationed there for the winter, I suppose; an order arrived about five this evening for the remainder of the soldiers to march; they hurried away, but returned in less than an hour, the officers thinking it too late for them to reach Bordentown to-night.

Jan. 8th. All the soldiers gone from the next house—only one of the number stopped to bid me farewell; but I did not resent it, remembering that only one of the ten lepers, cleansed by our Lord, returned to give thanks—not that I would compare the few trifling services I was enabled to render those poor creatures, to that great miracle; but it rose in my mind at the time, perhaps, as a check to any little resentment that I might have felt for being neglected. I went into the house after they had left it, and was grieved to see such loads of provisions wastefully lying on the floor. I sent my son to desire an officer in town to order it away, and he returned his compliments, and desired me " to keep it from spoiling "— that was, to make use of it; but as it was not his to give, and I had no stomach to keep it from spoiling, I sent it to another person, who had it taken to the sick soldiers.

Jan. 9th. We hear to-day that our troops have driven the English to Brunswick, and some say there has been another battle. All the officers went out of town to day. The report of poor A. Morris being killed, is confirmed by an officer who was in the battle. We hear that Washington has sent to buy up a number of stores, from whence it is concluded he is going into winter quarters. The weather very cold; some snow falling has also filled the river with ice, and we expect it will be strong enough to walk over in a day or two, and give an opportunity to those inclined to escape, of crossing over, which, for several weeks past, has been attended with some difficulty; all the boats belonging to the town being seized upon by the gentlemen of the galleys, and either borne away, or broke to pieces, which they said was done to prevent the Hessians from crossing the river: and, on the same pretence, a number of bridges have been taken up, and others so much damaged as to make it difficult for travellers to pass from hence to Philadelphia. Several of the soldiers, who were brought into town sick, have died, and it is feared the disorder by which they were afflicted is infectious.

Jan. 11th. Weather very cold, and the river quite shut. I pity the poor soldiers, now on their march, many of whom will probably lay out in the fields this cold night. What cause have I for gratitude, that I and my household are sheltered from the storm! oh that the hearts of my offspring may learn to trust in the God of their *mother*—He who has condescended to preserve us in great danger, and keep our feet from wandering from the habitation his goodness has allotted to us.

Jan. 12th. We are told to-day of the robbery of one of the commissaries—the sum lost is said to be £10.000. I have not heard who is suspected of committing the robbery. The Earl of B——n,* who quitted his habitation on the first alarm of the Hessians coming in, is returned with his family. We have some hopes that our refugee will be presented with a pair of lawn sleeves, when dignities become cheap, and suppose he will then think himself too *big* to creep into his old auger hole—but I shall remind him of the *place*, if I live to see him created first B——p of B——n.

*Ironical.—ED.

Jan. 13th. Several of the *tories*, who went out of town while the gondolas were here, are returned, on hearing there had been a general jail delivery at Philadelphia. One man, who thought himself immovable, has been compelled to swear or sign allegiance to the States.

Jan. 14th. The *lie* of the day runs thus—that the New England men have taken Long Island, are in possession of King's-Bridge—that Gen. Lee is retaken by his own men—the regulars in a desperate condition intrenching at Brunswick, and quite hopeless of gaining any advantage over the Americans this campaign. A letter from my amiable friend, E. C., informs me her husband's battalion was in the front of the battle at ———, and behaved remarkably well; they took 200 prisoners, and left 80 on the field; he acknowledges the preserving hand of Providence in bringing him safe through such a scene of blood, &c. I hear Gen. Howe sent a request to Washington, desiring three days' cessation of arms, to take care of the wounded, and bury the dead, which was refused; what a woful tendency war has to harden the human heart against the tender feelings of humanity! Well may it be called a *horrid art*—thus to change the nature of man. I thought that even barbarous nations had a sort of religious regard for their dead. A friend from Trenton tells me poor A. Morris died in three hours after he was wounded, and was buried in Friend's burying ground, at Stony Brook. Also Capt. Shippen was buried by him. The same friend told us that a man was killed in his bed at the house of Stacey Potts, at Trenton, in the time of the engagement there, and that Potts' daughter, about the age of mine, went from home to lodge, the night preceding the battle, and returning in the morning, just as she stepped into her father's door, a ball met her, (being directed by the unerring hand of Providence,) took the comb out of her hair, and gently grazed the skin of her head without doing her any further injury: who shall dare to say they are shot at random?

Jan. 15th. I was a good deal affected this evening, at seeing the hearse in which Gen. Mercer's body was conveyed over the river, on the ice, to be buried at Philadelphia; poor Capt. Shippen's body was also taken over, at the same time, to be reburied there. P. Reed gave us the following account of a report they heard from a man, whom her sister sent to Burlington to bring some things they were in want of the night the last soldiers came into town. Reed's wife hired a waggon to come here, and got one of her neighbours to come and fetch some of her goods. Just as the man began to load the wagon, the soldiers came running into town, and the man whipped up his horses and drove away without his goods. When he got to Reed's house in the country, he told them there was 10.000 wagons in Burlington—that Gen. Washington, Lee, Howe, and all the Americans were engaged in battle, in Burlington,—that Washington was mortally wounded, and the streets were full of dead bodies, and that the groans of the dying were still in his ears. They opened their letters in fearful haste, and found nothing relative to what the man told them, nor could they convince him that his fright had magnified the matter, till they sent a person up here to enquire.

* * A page of the MS. unfortunately missing.

Jan. 31st, 1777. The scruples of my own mind being satisfied in keeping my son here till the search was over, I felt peace in the prospect of sending him to my dear brother, C. M. (Dr. Charles Moore), and now that he is gone from me, I feel like a merchant who has ventured *half* his fortune out to sea, anxious for the success of the voyage; oh that it may be a prosperous one to my dear boy—then shall I be happy.

Feb. 3d. To day appeared in print, a proclamation of Gen. Washington's ordering all persons who had taken protections of the King's commissioners, to come in thirty days, and swear allegiance to the United States of America, or else, repair with their families to the lines of the British troops. What will become of our refugee, now!

Feb. 4th. To-day eight boats full of soldiers sailed up the river to join the continental forces; they appeared to be very merry with their drums beating, and colours flying; this is said to be the day appointed for our friends, who are prisoners, to have a hearing before Putnam; a man, who is not a lover of the peace, told us it was expected there would be bloody work on the occasion.

Feb. 6th. Several hundred soldiers, who were returning from the camp, were quartered on the inhabitants, and in general, I hear, behaved well.

Feb. 7th. All the soldiers quartered on the town last night, went away to-day. The prisoners taken from our town, and Mount Holly, discharged and returned home; several of them much fatigued, and some sick.

Feb. 11th. This evening two doctors were brought into town, and put into prison for inoculating in their families, contrary to the orders of Gen. Putnam, who had prohibited them from inoculating. They were discharged in a few days.

April 10th. Jno. Lawrence, Thomas Watson, and several other persons, obnoxious to the state, were imprisoned here, and divers others bound over to their good behaviour, and to appear at the next court—to be held—*nobody knows where.*

April 17th. A number of flat-bottomed boats went up the river, and landed troops at Bristol; it is said 1500 men are billeted on the inhabitants there.

April 19th. A report that there has been an engagement between the British troops and Americans; the latter victorious. B. Helm summoned before the governor, and bound to answer at the next court for preferring silver dollars to paper. The English said to be in motion, and the fleet below.

May 7th. Capt. Webb and his family came here in order to

set off the next day for New York, having received orders from the governor to depart the state. Just as they were retiring to bed, a captain of the light-horse arrived with a party of soldiers, and demanded the keys of his trunks—some of which they opened, and searched for letters, and took all they could find, and guarded him to his lodging, at R. Smith's, and were all night in his room: they set a guard over his goods, and in the morning returned and examined all his trunks, and then waited on him to Philadelphia, where he was to wait on the general, and answer to sundry charges, one of which was, that he was suspected of being a spy; this he boldly cleared himself of: another was, that he had in a sermon he preached, about two years ago, told the people that if they took up arms against the King, they would be d—d; he likewise pleaded innocent to this, and finding they could not prove it on him, they referred him to the governor, who reproved him for not taking advantage of a pass he had granted him, two or three weeks ago, and absolutely prohibited him from prosecuting his journey to York, and ordered him to repair with his family to Bethlehem, there to remain during their pleasure, and confined him to a magic circle of six miles.

May 10th. The court met here, when several persons, confined in our jail,—some tories,—were examined. Jno. Lawrence released; D. Ellis imprisoned, and J. Carty fined sixpence, for contempt of court; several ordered back to prison, and R. Smith, B. Helm, T. Hulings, and Collin Campbell examined; R. Smith ordered to pay £100, or be confined in prison; he chose the latter, and accordingly took possession of the room J. L. had quitted; the oaths offered to the three others, which they refusing, were fined.

May 26th. This day Capt. Webb and his family left us to go to Bethlehem. W. D., who some days since received a passport from Gen. Washington, set out for New York with the widow Allen.

June 7th.   The reports often coming by expresses, give us reason to believe the English army are in motion, and it is generally supposed they intend to bend their course to Philadelphia.

June 10th.   A person from the camp came to town to engage a number of guides (to go back with him,) who were well acquainted with the different roads to Philadelphia, that in case our people should be obliged to retreat, they may not be at a loss.

June 11th.   Certain intelligence arrived, per express, that the English are at Bound Brook, the Americans at Morristown.

June 13th.   Early this morning the soldiers beat to march from Bristol, and in the course of the day several boats full of soldiers, with the Pennsylvania militia, sailed up the river.

June 14th.   Before daylight this morning, the alarm guns, at Princeton, Trenton, Bordentown, and Bristol, were fired, and answered by those below ; about 9 o'clock the gondolas and barges began to appear in sight, and from that time, till 9 at night, there have gone up the river five or six gondolas.   Several flat-bottomed boats are also gone to Bristol.   There is a report of a battle to-day, which seems probable, as we have heard much firing above.   By a person from Bordentown, we hear twelve expresses came in there to-day from camp.   Some of the gondola men and their wives being sick, and no doctor in town to apply to, they were told that Mrs. M. was a skilful woman, and kept medicines to give to the poor ; and notwithstanding their late attempts to shoot my poor boy, they ventured to come to me, and, in a very humble manner, begged me to come and do something for them.   At first I thought they might have a design to put a trick upon me, and get me aboard of their gondola, and then pillage my house, as they had done some others ; but on asking where the sick folks were, was told they were lodged in the governor's house.   So I went to see them ; there were several, both men and women, very ill with a fever—some said the camp, or putrid fever ; they were broke out in blotches, and, on close examination, it appeared to be the itch fever. I treated them according to art, and they all got well. I thought I had received all my pay, when they thankfully acknowledged my kindness, but lo! in a short time afterwards, a very rough, ill-looking man, came to the door and asked for me; when I went to him, he drew me aside, and asked if I had any friends in Philadelphia; the question alarmed me, supposing there was some mischief meditated against that poor city; however I calmly said, I have an ancient father, some sisters, and other near friends there. "Well," said the man, "do you wish to hear from them, or send anything by way of refreshment to them—if you do, I will take charge of it, and bring you back anything you may send for." I was very much surprised, and thought, to be sure, he only wanted to get provisions to take to the gondolas, when he told me his wife was one of those I had given medicine to, and this was the only thing he could do to pay me for my kindness; my heart leaped with joy, and I set about preparing something for my dear absent friends. A quarter of beef, some veal, fowls, and flour, were soon put up, and about midnight the man called and took them aboard of his boat. He left them at Robert Hopkins's, at the Point, from whence my beloved friends took them to town, and, two nights after, a loud knocking at our front door greatly alarmed us. Opening the chamber window, we heard a man's voice, saying, "Come down softly and open the door, but bring no light;" there was something mysterious in such a call, and we concluded to go down, and set the candle in the kitchen—when we got to the front door, we asked "who are you?" the man replied, "a friend, open quickly;" so the door was opened, and who should it be but our honest gondola man, with a letter, a bushel of salt, a jug of molasses, a bag of rice, some tea, coffee, and sugar, and some cloth for a coat for my poor boys—all sent by my kind sisters. How did our hearts and eyes overflow with love to them, and thanks to our Heavenly Father, for such seasonable supplies. May we never forget it. Being now so rich, we thought it our duty to hand out a little to the poor around us, who were mourning for want of salt; so we divided the bushel and gave a pint to every poor person that came for it, and had a great plenty for our own use. Indeed it seemed as if our little store increased by distributing it, like the bread broken by our Saviour to the multitude, which, when he had blessed it, was so marvellously multiplied. One morning, having left my chamber at an earlier hour than usual, and casting my eyes towards the river, was surprised to see some hundreds of boats, all filled with British soldiers. I ran to my dear G. D.'s room, and begged him to get up and see the sight. He went to the window, and I waited to hear what he would say; but as he said nothing, I called out to him, "Brother, what shall we do, now?" He opened his door, and sweetly and calmly said, "Let us, my sister, keep still and quiet; I believe no harm will happen to us;" and indeed we were favoured with remarkable stillness; even the children seemed to partake of it. The boats were ordered up the river to Bordentown, to burn all the gondolas. Poor R. Sutton and his son passing my door, I stopped him, and asked him where he was going; he said, to join the soldiers to march to Bordentown, for the English were going to burn it, and on their return would do the same to Burlington. I begged him not to go, and said, perhaps he would be killed; he said he would go for all that—next day we heard he was killed. The report was, that some of the militia had fired on the English boats as they were rowing up the river; the firing was returned, and poor Sutton was the first, if not the only one killed; the last boat we saw, was a small one, with only three men and the rowers in it; they were not soldiers; when they came opposite to the town wharf, they stopped rowing, and pulled off their hats and bowed to the people on the wharf. We heard

afterwards it was our poor refugee, Dr. S. Burling, and J. Stans-
bury, who intended to have come on shore and paid us a visit, but
so many people appearing on the wharf they thought it safest to
take to their oars and follow the fleet. One large vessel, with
cannon, was in the fleet, and when they returned, were ordered to
fire if they saw soldiers on the wharf, or about the streets. It
seems the soldiers had notice of the time when they were to return, and they placed themselves along the shore, quite down to
the ferry ; it was First day afternoon, and all the family, but myself, gone to meeting, and I was laying on the bed, and hearing a
large gun, looked out of the window, and saw the large ship so
close to our landing that I thought they were coming ashore ; when,
behold ! they fired two or three of their great guns, which shook
the house, and went through the walls of our next door neighbour,
who was a captain in the rebel army. I still kept at the window,
unapprehensive of danger, and seeing a man on the deck talking,
and pointing to my house, one of them said, " In that house lives
a woman to whom I am indebted for my life ; she sheltered me
when I was driven from my own house," &c. This I was afterwards told by a person who heard it ; it is needless to add it was
our poor refugee. I really think they have made an end of the
gondolas ; I hope never to see another. A rebel quarter-master,
who had received some little civilities from my S. D. and myself,
asked me one day, if I did not wish to see my friends in Philadelphia ; I said it was the wish nearest my heart ; he said he would
accompany me as far as Frankfort, if I would promise to take no
kind of provision with me, and that he would meet me at the same
place, and conduct me home again. Such an offer was not to be
slighted—I went to my friend, A. O., and asked her if she would
venture to bear me company. She joyfully agreed, and we bor-
rowed a horse and chair, and early next morning set out. Our
quarter-master being our guard, and good neighbour J. V. went

with us to the ferry, to see us safe over. We got to A. James's place in the afternoon, and sent notice to our friends in town, and next morning my father, brothers, Moore and Wells, and my two sisters, with Dr. O. &c., met us at Kensington, for they dared not go further, that being the British lines. I believe there never was a more heart-tendering meeting. I had not seen my father and sisters for many months, and the dangers we were surrounded with, and the probability of this being the last time we might meet on earth, together with the reports of the great scarcity of provisions in town, and a thousand other things, all contributed to make it an awfully affecting meeting. My sisters went to A. J.'s place and dined with me. A. O. stayed with her husband till evening, when my dear sisters left me and returned to town. The parting was almost too much for me. I thought we were taking a last farewell of each other, but part we must ; they went to town, and Nancy and myself retired soon to bed, expecting our quarter-master to call on us by daylight, but no news did we hear of him ; but a heavy firing in the morning made us fearful we should not get safe home. About nine o'clock some stragglers stopped at our quarters, and said there had been a skirmish between the English and Americans, and, more terrible still, that parties were ordered out to bring in all they should meet with ; this intelligence made us conclude to venture homewards without our guide ; we got into our chair and whipped and cut our dull horse at a strange rate. Several parties passed and repassed, and questioned us about whence we came, and where we were going—they said if we were going to Burlington, we should be stopped at the ferry and taken to Washington's head quarters ; for there was a report that women had been into town and brought out goods. We kept our minds pretty calm, hoping that if we got safe to the ferry, as we were so well known, we should meet no more dangers, and we got along well till we got to the hill beyond the Red Lyon, which being very bad, and we still pressing our poor horse to make more haste, he made one violént exertion to reach the top of the hill, when, to our utter dismay, the swingletree broke, and the chair began to roll down the hill. We both jumped out at the same instant; Nancy held the horse while I rolled a stone behind the wheel, and there we stood afraid to stir from the horse, and thinking we should be obliged to leave the chair, and lead the horse home. At last we ventured to the door of a small house hard by; a man came out, and with the help of Nancy's ribbons and my garters, fixed us off, and we once again mounted the chair, and walked the horse till we came near the Bristolroad, where we heard the ferry was guarded, and none suffered to cross. However we kept on, and at length reached the ferry, where, instead of armed men, we could hardly find one man to put us over. At last we got over, and now being on our own shore, we began like people just escaped from shipwreck, to review the dangers past, and congratulate ourselves on our arrival in a safe port; and I hope not without a sincere, though silent, acknowledgment of the good hand that had vouchsafed to bring us so far on our way to our lonely habitations. When we arrived at my door, my beloved S. D. had the neighbours and children all sitting with her; her tender anxious mind filled with apprehensions for our safety. As we had stayed a day longer than we intended, it was conjectured by our wise neighbour, J. V., that some terrible thing had happened, nothing less than that the horse, which was his, had been seized, and we kept in Pennsylvania. Rd. Smith, who lent the chair, was equally alarmed for the fate of his carriage; and S. H., who loudly exclaimed against the expedition, said we were certainly carried to head quarters; and as Nancy's husband was in the British pay, it would go hard with her for his sake; but, behold! all their wise conjectures proved like the croaking of the raven, for in the midst of it all, we appeared before them in our proper persons, before our arrival was announced. Some cried out, where's the horse? where's the chair? where have you been? &c. We gaily told them all was safe, then sat down to a good dish of tea, and rehearsed all we had seen, heard, and suffered; when we were seriously advised never to engage again in such a perilous undertaking; and we as seriously assured them that if we did we would look out for a stronger horse and chair, and be our own guide, for that our late expedition, so far from being a discouragement, was like a whet to an hungry man, which gave him a better appetite for his dinner.

Finis